Whispers, Screams, and Crying Out Loud

Poems, Prayers, and Essays to Help You
Find, Feel, And Trust Your Voices,
Your Truths.

Paula Strupeck Gardner, M.A., M.A.

Copyright © 2023, Paula K. Strupeck Gardner

All rights reserved. No part of this publication may be reproduced, distributed, or transmitted in any form or by any means, including photocopying, recording, or other electronic or mechanical methods, without the prior written permission of the publisher, except in the case of brief quotations embodied in reviews and certain other non-commercial uses permitted by copyright law.

> To request permissions, contact the author at:
> email: paulaksgardner@gmail.com
> website:www.paulaksgardner.com

1st Edition: March, 2023
ISBN: 978-1-7352276-2-7 (Paperback)

This volume of poems, prayers, and essays has been shared over the years with my students and clients from around the world.

To receive YOUR free recording of one of Paula's readings and to join her email community,

Go to:
www.YourVoicesYourTruths.com

Dedication

*I share this book—and all its being—
with profound gratitude:*

To Susan, *for calling me a Renaissance woman;*
To Julie Ann, *for helping me see The Renaissance Woman that I am;*
To Jacqueline, *for helping me be The Renaissance Woman that I am;*
To Me, *for embodying the Renaissance Woman that I am;*
To my Angels, *for bringing it all to the surface.*

Gratitude is the grace of receiving all the beauty that is.

Table of Contents

Introduction 9

Words Spoken From the Heart Enter the Heart. 13
Dal Cuore di Paola 14
Your Words and Me 16
Stillness Speaks 19
A Trilogy 20
And the Greatest of These is Love 21
Misplacing My Voice 22
Screaming is Meditation, Too! 26
Whose Voice? (Which of my voices are you?) 28
Why Weight? 30
The Miracles We Are 36
Speaking Our Truths 38
Embracing Who We Are 43
For Karen H. 46
The Songs of Our Soul 48
Beyond Words 50
I Can See Clearly Now… 52
Try These On 55
Editing 57
Feeling ALL of the Feelings, Even the Unpretty Ones 59
Just Sayin' 63
Death's Smile 67
Feeling and Trusting the Feelings… 69

What's in YOUR Wallet? 74
A Practice of Time 77
A Practice of Time Part Two 78
Brilliance 79
Whose Voice Do You Hear? 81
Club Baseball 83
When I'm Invited and I Cannot / Do Not Want To 84
Blocking Out the Other Voices 85
Crying in the Shower Version 604A 86
Traveling Light 89
When the Pelvis Leads 92
Finding My Voices 95
What Does A Woman Who Feels Worthy Do? 99
Beauty Hunter 106
Echoes 109
Manifesto/Io Credo (I believe. I know.) 112

Closing Notes 119
Acknowledgements 121
About the Author 123

Introduction

"All holiness is about hearing the voice of your own soul."
— *John O'Donohue*

"If words come from the heart, they will enter the heart."
— *Rumi.*

"Words are things, I'm convinced… Someday we'll be able to measure the power of words. I think they are things. I think they get on the walls, they get in your wallpaper, they get in your rugs, in your upholstery, in your clothes. And, finally, into you."
— *Dr. Maya Angelou*

I have lots of words in my head.
I have lots of voices in my head.
Some of them have been with me my whole life and come from the outside.
Some of them were there before me — the ancestral voices embedded in our DNA that can haunt us, can lift us up, can crush us, can enable, embolden and enrich us.
Some of these voices I imagined and put there all on my own because of how I interpreted the voices swirling around me.

It's all real. It all counts.
We are the sum of our experiences.
We are MORE than the sum of our experiences.
We are what we make of these experiences, how we interpret them, the meaning we give them.
We are what we are at birth and beyond.

We give meaning to the voices around us we give meaning to our own voices.

And we have many, don't we?

We have this idea sometimes that we must use the same voice, be the same person across all the roles we play in our life.

How can this possibly be true? real?

We have a voice for each of the roles we play in life—mother, father, sister, brother, daughter, son, teacher, gardener, business owner, team player, athlete, worker, leader, follower, dancer, singer, accountant, etc.

We have a voice for the little person we were (and who lives inside us still and whom we need to care for).

We have a voice for the person we are becoming (who lives inside us and is happy to lead us to them).

And when we stand up and say, "I," we empower ourself in untold, unimagined, unforeseen ways.

This is a book of standing up and saying, "I."

Sometimes, boldly and bravely.
Sometimes, with great trepidation and doubt.
Sometimes, nonchalantly and matter-of-factly.
Sometimes, in deep grief.
Sometimes, in utter joy.
Sometimes, speaking from fear;
other times from great confidence.
Sometimes, doing so even though I'm terrified of what might happen,
what others might think, how I might be punished,
how I might punish myself.
And sometimes, I keep my voice quiet or even silent… because…
I'm human.

These are a FEW of all the voices within.

I used to think I needed to direct my life to finding my one, singular voice.
I now believe firmly that I'm finding all my voices that make up this singularity and that I will continue to do so throughout my life.

Just as our physical voice changes and grows as we change from child to teen to young adult to adult to older adult;
Just as our "voice," our perception of how things are, changes as we grow from child to teen to young adult to adult to older adult;
Our voice shifts as we live our life.

And all these voices remain in our mind-body-spirit,

guiding us, warning us, loving us when we let them.

Please. Let's let them.

This is a collection of things I've written.
When I reread them, I hear the voice of the girl/woman who wrote the words.
Sometimes, I read them in today's voice in order to reassure that girl that I heard and saw her.
Sometimes, I read today's words in the little girl voice so she can feel what she's become.

Sometimes, I wonder what the words sound like in another's voice.
Do you read them aloud?
Do they resonate in your heart of hearts?
When this happens, I feel deeply gratified that I have shared the words and that you feel at home with them, that you feel safe and sacred with them. And I feel deeply grateful when you share with me that my words resonate in and through your voice.

Please join my online community and share YOUR voices with ours. Enter your name at www.YourVoicesYourTruths.com and receive a FREE recording of selections from this book. I look forward to welcoming you!

Words Spoken From the Heart Enter the Heart

What we say matters
and how we say what we say matters.

We can decide to make each word, phrase, tone of voice

A prayer

Just as we can decide to make each smile, grimace, glide, dance,
Stumble, fall,
Rise…

A prayer.

Just as we can make of our day, our night, our afternoon;
Just as we can make of our life;
Just as we can make of our self

A prayer.

We can speak from our heart
and enter the heart of every person around us.

We can make each one of them

A prayer.

Blessings Always,

Paula

Dal Cuore di Paola

One of my favorite chants comes from the Taittirya Brahmana. It is a much longer chant (Laghunyasah) that is performed during one's daily washing,
where the gods are invited to cleanse, restore, and elevate each body part to serve the greater good. It is a prayer to link body, senses, energy, mind, and awareness.

Atma hrdaye hrdaye mayi. Aham amryte amritam anandam Bhramhani

Traditional translation: My true nature is the heart. The heart is my true nature. I am the bliss of the heart.

My interpretation:
I speak from my heart; I teach from my heart; I write and dance and live from my heart.
My heart is one with yours.

I've shared this chant at the end of yoga classes, during gong sessions, healing bowl practices. I've chanted it to myself to help me feel safe, or comforted, or trusting.
I've chanted it to remind myself that who I am—the being who lives from her heart—is beautiful.
I've chanted it alone.
I've chanted it with others.
I've taught it in the traditional call and response ways.

Please go to: htttps://bit.ly/3Zx2GXx and chant with me!

Let me know how it feels in YOUR voice!

Your Words and Me

Your words…
Cut me
Slice me
Carry me to a dark, darker, darkest
Moment/place

Your voice…
Drips with rage and wrath

I cannot help
(because of me, because of the moment, because of you,
because of history, because of ancestry, because of life)
I cannot help
But feel
It's meant for
And is about me.

And I quake
In my bones
And sinew
And muscle.
Bodily fluids
Carry
The vibrations
Of your hostility
Far and wide
Within me

I receive them.
I make them about me
I let their waves rock me to and fro
Until they become mine;
Become me.

Please don't shout so loud.
Please don't glare so hard.
Please don't feed my fragile heart
with the leftovers of love unlived.

Please see in my eyes
The terror in my heart.

And revise and edit and monitor

And remember
I'm listening
Even when you're not.
Sometimes,
We speak from our angry heart
Without knowing
Without seeing
Without appreciating

The depths to which our words and voice
Sink the ships of spirits
Within hearing distance
Within feeling distance

Sometimes,
Without knowing,

We let out the layers of the hurt
In our life
And hurt the layers of hearts
Around us.

Sometimes,
Without knowing…

Now we know

So stop.
So look.
So listen
To the hearts around you.

Let their eyes remind you
To speak and look and listen
From the layers of love.

Stillness Speaks

Wait a minute.
Just one minute.
Only one minute.

Pause to sit for 1 minute.
Pause for 1 minute
Before you speak
To yourself.

In that pause,
You'll re-find,
Re-visit
Re-align yourself with love.

Pause and invite awareness in.

One minute changes your world.

A Trilogy

Do this with me. (Go to https://bit.ly/439cGtk for the video.)

Rub your hands rigorously together
To generate some heat.

Cup your hands gently over your eyes.

Receive the warmth from your hands
In your eyes
In their sockets
In your cheeks, your jaw, your throat,
All the way down to your heart.

Pause.

Place a smile
Behind your eyes,
Behind your lips,
Behind your heart.

Feel, receive and then share the softness
That moves
Into your thoughts,
Your words,
Your actions.

And the Greatest of These is Love

Find your strength.
Feel your strength.
Trust your strength.
Live in your strength.

Return to your strength when it wavers, when it falters.

When your strength seems gone, know that it remains in
 your heart of hearts
to guide you on your path,
to your path,
to keep your wisdom,
to fold you in the arms of love.

For LOVE IS our greatest strength.

Misplacing My Voice

Brilliant.
Beautiful.
Blonde.
Witty and charming.
Passionate.

I see her on book covers
and in interviews
and the light in me dims
to blackness,
to my darkness that plagues me,
has shadowed me since my childhood
of hearing tales of those who have (them)
versus those who have not (us),
tales of needing to be better than or
ending up as less-than.

Competition for affection,
for attention,
for love
defined my childhood into young adulthood…
into now…

Unknowingly, unwittingly,
I stuck those beliefs into my pocket
and held them as my own
and they have served the purpose

of holding me in their death grip,
isolating me from those deemed more worthy than I
of recognition,
of praise,
of contracts,
of popularity,
of attention,
of wealth,
of renown,
of … you name it…..

I read on,
I continue to listen,
nonetheless,
and each chapter
slams me
as a reflection of how unworthy I feel
since I am NOT
brilliant. beautiful. blonde.

Blessed Mother, Holy Spirit, Lord Jesus,
All the Angels and Saints and Holy Men, Women, and
    Children,
Please hand me the torch,
my torch,
the light that is me.

Guide my steps around and across the debris
scattered here, there
all around and in my eyes, my heart, my being
that believe that she…

oh, honestly…that ALL
have gifts
beyond mine,
gifts that merit
being read, listened to,
shared.

Pass me, please, the bucket to quell
the flames of resentment, jealousy…
weeds that grew from a childhood of
hearing those tales of the haves versus we who have not,
weeds that choked the flowers
neglected
because they weren't what the others grew or wore or had
and, therefore, were not beautiful, brilliant of their own
    being.

You have granted me the persistence to continue on
in the privacy of my own scared, but sacred space,
to write, to breathe life into these scattered words of feelings
and put them on paper to bring them to the light of day.

Grant me now the faith to share them
because they speak also of others'
fears, sadness, resentments, loss…and hope.

In their space on the page,
they water this hope,
solidarity, union,
the understanding that we are not alone.
We are neither less than
nor more than.

We are one.

Our ideas and passions
intersect, overlap, complement.
Our voices resonate with different folks
of different ages, of different stripes,
all having this common soul.

Beyond being brilliant. beautiful. blonde.

We are one.
And together, we are
fearless.

Together, we are free.

Together, our words shore up
the thousands, millions, billions of souls
who ache to see and feel their grace,
their light,
their sweetness,
their love
and how they are loved.

We are one.
All of us.

Brilliantly
Beautifully
One.

Screaming is Meditation, Too!

Our vision of meditation can be very restrictive.
I know it has been for me:
Sitting on a cushion for hours on end,
Gaze fixed.
Mind still.
Voice quiet.

What if…

What if everything we participate in could be our
 meditation?

What if we brought our full presence into our life
And fixed our heart's gaze on this moment?
On our self in this moment?
On the person in front of in this moment?

What if we acknowledged, then silenced all the inner critics
And all our real and imagined nemeses
And gave our self over to the voices
Within us
That needed to SCREAM in this moment?

What if the collections of pain and mortifications and
Grief and embarrassment and shame and sorrow
And disappointment
All culminated into large-mouthed NOISE

That racked our chest and led our eyes to stream with their
Deep loneliness and rage and profound longing?

What if SCREAMING is a meditation too?

What if, in fully participating in this powerful version of our
    voice,
In joining with our body in this ritual of release,
We free our self to breathe and be
Even more fully present in this moment?

I embrace this message that Tahnee shared:

Screaming is meditation, too.

Whose Voice?
(Which of my voices are you?)

I see the girl
In her ice blue silky gown
With the matching ice blue boa-lined
Hooded jacket.

She's leaning across the table,
Pointing with an inexpertly manicured finger to…?

One might believe that she's
Gesturing with pride at the poem,
Her poem,
That is featured in the school's dance program,
Bids they called them.

I listen more closely.
She is, rather, pointing to an error-
Of editing or hers?
It's uncertain.

She's been published before
But her words
Had been altered to
Match the editor's ideas
Of beauty and cohesion,
Of rhythm and grace

And so misrepresented
Their composer's
Intentions,
Origins…

Voice.

Whose voice is this girl in ice blue hearing in this tableau?

Hers? Theirs?
The Collective's?
The Imagined?
The Anticipated?
The Feared?

All of the above?
None of the above?

Which multiple choice most reflects her realities?
Her fears?
Her desires?

Which multiple choice will she opt to believe in?
I know who I'm cheering for.

You?

Why Weight?

I saw a video of myself made a year ago…

before I gained 25 pounds.

My initial reaction was: "I look so much thinner." And then I looked more closely and I honestly didn't know if I really looked thinner or if my judging brain assumed that I looked thinner because the scale tells me today that I weigh 25 pounds more than I did then.

This "how much do you/I weigh" has plagued me for…oh, most of my life.

I watched my mother go up and down the scale. No…I watched my mother have more flesh, less flesh, more again. I listened to her talk a lot about weight and diets and losing weight.

I joined her when I was a little girl on the floor when she exercised with Gloria on WGN.

And even now, at age 99, she bemoans her weight, her appearance as heavy.

Judge. Criticize. Repeat.

Why?

Why weight?

Why do we do this to ourselves? Men and women. Especially women, though.

What is it about our sense of self that so relies on an arbitrary number on a scale to tell us whether we are good?

Why do we inversely measure our worth by how much we weigh? The higher the number, the less we appreciate, embrace, enjoy, love ourself.

I've denied it, hidden it and hidden from it in myself. I've pretended that it didn't matter to me (I even moved the scale to another room so it wasn't taunting me every single morning.). I encouraged other people to not pay attention to it (at the same time encouraging myself). I've loved and love bigger others with an open heart but as MY clothes get smaller and tighter, I get smaller in my mind and heart about what's happening. I can feel my insides shrinking from…shame? disappointment? discouragement? fear?

I get judge-y about that 2nd slice of delicious, just-out-of-the-oven homemade bread, slathered with butter.

I deride myself about the size of the portions I eat (too big), about my enjoyment of everything food (too strong, too excessive).

Several situations are in play in this moment that have me squirming and squiggling with discomfort:

One of my sons is eating vegan.

I gained about 25 pounds over the last year in ways and places I've not experienced before…and it's not going anywhere.

I'm 64 years old. My metabolism is different than it was even 10 years ago. I'm not as active as I was even 2 years ago.

I'm wrestling with aging or rather my fears and thoughts and anxieties about aging.

I want to age with grace and vitality and lovingkindness, with strength of mind, body, and spirit, with my beauty hunter-ness intact and fierce. I want to be vibrant and dynamic in my body/mind/spirit's wisdom.

And I want to be present with and at peace with the changes that come as they come. I want to be wise and centered, joyful and at peace.

So I regularly (daily) ask myself:

Does it matter what the scale says if I'm able to walk in my beloved woods and along the ocean til I die?

NO!

How does a number matter to whether or not I can crawl on the floor with my grandkids (I don't have any yet—just so you know and don't get excited for me.) or make music with them or play in the waves with them? How does a number matter to traveling with my sons and their families as they grow?

It doesn't.

What is magic about 3 digits that makes me feel younger, more attractive, more desirable (Studies do show that attractive people get hired more readily.) when I'm on my way to wisdom and not working or mating?

Nothing!

As I slide towards old,
how do I best let go of the deeply engrained sense that only youth matters, that once beyond youthful, we decrease in worth?

I certainly embrace OTHERS in THEIR age and wisdom. Why do I withhold this deference and respect and admiration from myself?

How do I get comfortable with more flesh, increasing need for rest, greater need for targeted effort in strength training, with a deepening and expanding recognition of time passing and of my role changing and growing, NOT diminishing?

It's my journey. Perhaps yours, too?
Can we share what we learn or have learned so far?
Can we walk this crooked path together?

I recognize that we're each on our own stairway to heaven.

Macrina Wiedekehr (the Benedictine Sister) says, "heaven is here on earth" when we practice being totally present in our self in each moment.

This is my focus right now, more than ever:
Be present with ALL of it, with all of me.

"Let me see the truth about myself, no matter how beautiful it is." the brilliant Macrina Wiedekehr again.

Let me look at myself in the mirror and—instead of scrunching up my face in horror at the extra flesh, at the wrinkles at my throat, at the disappearing eyebrows—let me recognize and love that the smiles and laughter lived remain forever etched on my face.

Let me see with loving eyes that the bright colors I choose to wear (in defiance at this point) draw my spirit out into the world in a rainbow of delight.

Let me ease into my old age, continuing to love and delight in the vibrancy of the world around and in me. Let me appreciate that this is so BECAUSE I understand the world is one and I understand this because of who I am and because of how old this who-I-am is.

Let me practice patience with myself and others. It has been forever in short supply.
Let me practice quiet moments and pauses throughout my day.
Let me practice whatever kind of yoga I can muster at any given moment of any given day.
Let me practice lovingkindness of myself as well as others.
Let me do the strength training necessary to build myself to whatever level I'm able in order to shore up whatever crumbling may take place in this body preparing for the latter parts of life.

Let me proceed with as much confidence and physical strength as I can create and feed in order to embrace and celebrate the wonder and awe of every day life.

It's not the weight on the scale that matters, is it?

It's the weight we carry in our mind and in our heart "until" we begin to shed those pounds and allow ourself to move freely and lovingly and joyfully, to see ourself with loving eyes…no matter what.

Let's help each other shed those "pounds" that weigh heavily in our mind and heart, let's help each other see ourself with loving eyes, and to do all that we can to move freely and lovingly and joyfully through our days and nights!

You in?

Blessings Always,

Paula

The Miracles We Are

Such a magnificent world we live in.

I glance out—
Over the clouds
The sea of blue sky
Dazzles

I'm reminded
Of the miracle of flight,
The miracle of human ingenuity,
Fueled by the Divine within and around us.

In remembering the Divine within,
I smile,
Comfortable in the knowing,
Inspired by the knowing,
Surrounded by the knowing.

Stop..
With open eyes
With open heart
With mind attuned to serving its heart.

Look.

Listen
With open ears,

With open heart
With mind attuned to serving its heart.

We are the miracle
We make more miracles with what and who we are.

Speaking Our Truths

How we see things comes from lots of places inside us, doesn't it?
And how we express these things we see can show us a great deal about how we've come to this place of speaking our truth.

Consider this:
When we feel at ease in our self,
when we trust ourself and our perceptions just because they are ours,
we can express ourself clearly, concisely, even gently or lovingly because we feel no need to defend or protect ourself.

Our voice reflects the depth to which we trust ourself;
it reflects a softness, perhaps, that shows that we are still willing to listen to others' voices at the same time that we are comfortable in sharing ours.

When we feel at ease in our thoughts and words and feelings, we don't feel a need to prove ourself or persuade another.
Our tone of voice reflects the musical instrument that the voice is.
Our words are lyrical, even loving.

We simply state what we see, how we feel.

As a Senior in college,
I took a course in Medieval French literature.

It was an Independent Study.
The Professor was deeply excited that SOMEone wanted to read and discuss
Medieval French literature, her passion.

One of the themes—miracles—
was already one of *my* life themes.

But I took what turned out to be a very different approach from the standard, prescribed perspective of miracles as the professor believed them and had studied them to be.

And she was greatly dismayed at how tenaciously I defended my belief that miracles were found in every day life.

No matter how much evidence I produced from the literature, she was adamant that I was wrong.

It wasn't that my perspective was different.
She CERTAINLY wasn't celebrating that my perspective was unique or that she had never seen it that way.

No.
I was simply, utterly wrong.

I look now at several episodes in my life in academia
where I steadfastly stood by the insights that arrived in my mind/heart as I read or wrote assignments.

I stood my ground.
And yet, the episodes chipped away at the strength of my voice.

The chipping away continued the job that had begun when I was a younger child.

I saw things differently.
Others made my perspectives wrong.
And so I learned to defend before I even shared.
I learned to come out fighting.

This is very wearing, of course.
And fatigue makes us vulnerable to suggestions,
especially those suggestions that come from our nervous system's instincts to save and protect us.

Those suggestions tend to be things like:
Who do you think you are?
What makes you think you can do that?
What makes you think that you know more than she does?
What makes you think you can trust yourself?
What makes you think you're worthy?

These kinds of questions insinuate themselves into the core of our being and sabotage our efforts, our dreams, our joy. We're not aware of them. And what we are not aware of controls our life.

Over the last couple of years, I've been devotedly practicing self reiki with the intention to see where all this came from (to become aware) so that I may ease the fears that hold me back from loving, being, breathing deeply.

And wow! the memories spill over and in and through. I can't write fast enough!

But wow too!
It's been so incredibly helpful and healing and relieving and inspiring and…!

I undertook this journey—if you will—NOT as a way to shame or blame the people in my life who behaved this way.
But to help me understand how these are not me.

To help me see myself with loving eyes so that I could see it all and not turn away from the "dark" sides.
To help me embrace me.
To help set me back on the track
of listening to and trusting my ways of seeing things, my ways of being,
of listening to and trusting my voices.
of listening to and trusting my Inner Knowing.
of listening to and trusting that I am worthy.

How I see things is based on how I am.
And how I am sees life as a miracle—every day, every way, every thing in every day.

And the medieval French authors?
They agree with me! They saw miracles in every tree limb, every leaf, every rain drop, every coincidence, every gesture, ever loving word, every kindness, every speck of dirt…because they saw the Divine in every teeny tiny thing.

Your eyes are filled with miracles too.
Your voice is filled with the wonders of you—the dark, the light, the in between, the sweetness, the sour, the loving, the angry, the grieving…

All of this you is a wonder, is a miracle.

So, I beg you: Allow no one else's certainty or doubt to cast a shadow over or into your voice.
Speak YOUR truth because the world needs YOUR voice to speak YOUR thoughts and YOUR feelings, whether they agree with the sages, the experts, the professors, the parents or not.

We need YOU.
We need YOUR voices.

Blessings Always,
Paula

Embracing Who We Are

One thing I learned from my time with The Boy
Was to trust my perceptions…

Although I didn't exercise this trust with him directly.
Or even soon after.
But in the revisiting, the retelling, the recognition,
I see and I learn because I did NOT trust then.

My challenging encounter with the professor
Of medieval literature
Came during the time I dated The Boy and may even have been related to his and my conversations about all manner of things that HE felt strongly about.

He felt unappreciated for his genius in school.
He saw actions and activities from a perspective different from what I'd grown up with.

For the first time, I questioned my own experiences.
I looked at my time in grammar school with a more critical eye.
First and 2nd grade, I was way ahead in learning what other kids were learning so I was assigned to be their tutor.

I never thought about it.
I was a helper.

Through The Boy's eyes, I saw it as usurping my brilliance,

Derailing it really, undermining my intelligence because I wasn't being allowed, encouraged, supported to go further in my work. I was being "Used" to help the others.

For a while, (as in for years following these conversations, long after The Boy and I had parted ways—he dumped me—Thank God!), I was angry that I'd not been allowed to develop my intellectual prowess (as a 7-year-old, this was, of course, of primary importance).

Then, as I studied learning styles, I felt conflicted and somewhat guilty and defensive of the good Sister who had 50 children in her care and saw me as a golden opportunity for those needing extra help to get help.

I recognized then the possibility that in helping others, I was reinforcing my own learning, deepening it, refining it, expanding it beyond my life to learn about and appreciate my capacity as well as others'.

It fed my view of myself as a helper.

I felt a need to defend this view of myself.

Today, I have no answers to those questions of intellectual development.

Today, I have a clear appreciation of myself as a helper.

I'm proud to be one of those people spoken of admiringly by Mr. Rogers, "Look for the helpers. There are always helpers."

I don't raise my hand to be called on.

I step in.

Blessings,
Paula

For Karen H.

When you are truly yourself, you inspire others to be truly themself.

This was Karen for me (and probably others as well).
Together, we had a wicked sense of humor.
She did. And so, in her presence, mine felt free to be.
We made people laugh out loud.
We cried we laughed so hard.

When you are wholly who you are, you help others shine their light from being wholly who they are.

This was Karen for me (and probably others as well).
Together, we honored our profound adoration of our children.
No political agendae.
No trying to pretend that we were cool in our dealings with our children.
We simply and utterly adored them,
Giving others the permission to love their own children out loud.

When you have shed the veils of pretending to be other than you are, you grant to everyone around you the freedom to be who they are.

This was Karen for me (and probably others as well).

Together, we stood tall and proud in all we were and all we
   chose and all we did.
She did. And so, in her presence, I felt free to breathe and
   be…me.

Thank God,
I have a heart full of memories of all the strength, insight,
   steadfastness, caring, laughter,
you brought to my life.

While I shall miss you forever,
you live on
every time I am true to me,
every time I honor myself,
every time I laugh out loud,
every time I act generously,

every time I breathe and be me,
I shall be honoring your influence in my life.

Friends into Forever.

The Songs of Our Soul

Your voice.
Your rhythm.
Your timing.
Your lyrics.
Your melody.

Our words are the song of our soul.

Which song from your song book, from your far-reaching
    repertoire
Are you choosing to sing in this moment?

Are you conducting
Are you even listening
To how the notes

Are hurting people's ears?

Are you choosing your play list
Or are you mindlessly
Aimlessly repeating
Someone else's play button
As though it were your own?

Your voice is the instrument of your soul.
You get to use your voice
To reflect your deepest, truest self

And all the layers in between
OR

You get to be played by the world
Of the world's whim
Rather than you choosing.

BUT…you're read these words now
And
Once you're aware,
You can't go back to sleep or blindness or deafness.

Beyond Words

I read a book…
Where the author describes in detail
The stories spoken to her
By ancient trees.

I felt bereft.
I love trees.
They don't speak to me
Or if they do,
I don't know the words they use
So I think they're not talking to me.

Instead, I feel like there's something wrong with me
that I can't understand the words of the trees.

Here's what I FEEL from the trees, though.

Welcomed.
Rooted via their roots
Inspired to feel, cultivate, settle and share my own roots
    because mother trees share everything with all the
    plants and beings around them—no matter the genus or
    species
Reassured when feeling lonely or scared or at-odds-with
Listened to
Heard
Seen

Felt (When I allow myself)
Schooled in the best possible ways by their Presence that
    remind me of my intrinsic value to the world,
Of my beauty,
Of my grace,
Of my intelligence,
Of my love,
Of my loveliness as. I. Am.
Not what. I. Do. (Though this matters, it's not the be-all-end
    all of me)

Beyond words, they tell me.

We are beyond words.

I Can See Clearly Now...

Back in November, my friend and mentor Jacqueline Gates had exhorted us to clean all the mirrors and glass surfaces in our homes so that we could enjoy clearer vision headed into the New Year. I believe it had something to do with being in Scorpio.

I faithfully did mirrors, picture frames, table tops, but did only a cursory cleaning of the one mirror that has plagued me ever since my sons—when little boys—decorated my mirror with their favorite stickers. I was touched by their care and left them there…oh, too long.

Now, each time I clean this particular mirror, the little nurbles (which I believe are from the glue) persist and, most of the time, I tell myself, "I'll get it when I have more time." Hah.

We all know when that happens.

But yesterday, as I was replacing dead lightbulbs around the house,
I came face to face with this mirror—the mirror I look into when I brush my teeth, when I do my eye brows, when I….It's mine.

Jacqui talks about making our "chores" into rituals.
And I've begun intending to do one nice thing each day for my home.

So my mirror became the metaphor for my intention for 2016 of seeing my purpose more clearly. Of illuminating.

I wrote this in my journal to begin 2016.

2016. Illuminate. See clearly: I as I am. Them as they are. Us as we are. Things as they are. The past. The present. The future as I intend to create it.

BUT….

How could I see my purpose when I have glue-y nurbles on my mirror?

I began at the top so that I could see clearly into the stars where I'm aiming.
As I grew tired of scraping my thumbnail against the surface of the mirror (no other fingernail worked!), I began making rationalizations and excuses…

As long as I can see clearly into the stars, I have a chance, right?
The ones, the nurbles, right in my face (my present) I'll look around and past.
I can do that, right?!

NO! Do them ALL!

And when I can see clearly in the present,
I'll be better able to see clearly into the stars.

What about the ones near the bottom, the really stubborn ones?

My past, my friends.

All the sticky, gummy, gooey memories and scars of hurts and misunderstandings and mean-nesses suffered (and committed). If I don't let them go, how will I be able to see clearly who I was? where I came from? who I am now?

And who I intend to be?

So I scraped. And I scraped and I spritzed and I scraped.

The nurbles are gone now.
The bottom, center, and top of the glass are
clear and clean.

The past, the present, the future.

2016. Illuminate. See all as it was, is, will be.

I can see clearly now.

Happy New Year!

Blessings,
Paula

Try These On

Step into the shoes
To feel how you feel in them—
Physically, mentally, emotionally, spiritually.

Step into the shoes
And try on the self that wears these shoes
How does she see and feel about you?
Is she inviting you or directing you elsewhere?
Where does she go in these shoes?
What's she wearing when she wears these shoes?
What's she doing when she wears these shoes?
What words does she say when she wears these shoes?

Step into the shoes
And notice what changes in your layers of self
From outside to inside
And back again.

Where are you right here right now?
In which layer are you residing? Resting? Stuck?
Which shoes do you WANT to wear to get where you want
    to be?
Which shoes fit that layer?
Fit today?
Which shoes are good for this moment
And meant to be a passing fancy,
A moment of unbridled frivolity and joy?

Of connection with THIS layer of you
As part of you and quite festive
And not designed for every day wear

Except…

You can carry this part in your heart
And express her

WithOUT these shoes

Because this joie de vivre is in YOU,
And not in the shoes.

It's you.

All you.

Editing

A word or two on editing.
Censuring

To edit, one must have the work in front of you, completed.

All too often,
We say "write without editing"
As though we could edit while we write.

When the words are aspiring to my pen
And I cross them out,
Am I editing or am I censoring?

Today, I see this approach to "editing" as censoring
Inhibiting, blocking, denigrating? Me.

Don't do that.
don't censor yourself

You're so totally worthy of
Putting it all on paper,
Of living unscripted,
Of singing unrehearsed,
Of writing, uncensored.

You're so totally worthy
Of living out loud

Of living out soft
Of living out silence
Of living out laughter
Of living out crying
Of living out loving

You're so totally worthy.
You so totally are.

Feeling ALL of the Feelings, Even the Unpretty Ones

Are you tired of all this conversation about rage?
Or is it as new for you as it is for me and so we'll just keep exploring!

It intrigues me,
Especially since I got feedback that my words resonated…
AND that I should know better than to feed rage.

That last one intrigued me as much as the first.

Feeling the feelings
means feeling ALL the feelings…

and this includes those feelings that we were once told are BAD.

That was the old word.

The new word(s) for telling us that the feelings are bad includes telling us that if we aspire to service and caring, then anger, rage, or anything other than peace and love are beneath us.

Another way is to say that it's unbecoming.

Or self-indulgent.

Or ugly.

Another thing we do is to bypass the ugliness so that we can embrace
the letting go, the moving beyond, the healing.

BALDERDASH!

YOU CAN'T HEAL WHAT YOU CAN'T FEEL.

Oooo…I like the sound of this:

You can't heal what you can't/don't/won't feel.

I guided a beautiful retreat last weekend with 10 women who made the retreat beautiful.

At the last minute, I added a practice of acknowledging and addressing rage as a way to access softness.

Think about it: If we're harboring rage (our feelings—especially the unacknowledged feelings—nestle into our muscles and stay there until we look at them and do something for them), we are very limited in the softness that we can invite, receive, and feel.

And I shared this story:
When my younger son was born, the older son was not quite two years old.
Younger son was 6 weeks early and I spent a week in the hospital before he was born.
The day after he arrived, my husband brought son #1 to visit.

He sat on my lap, looked me right in the eye and began snapping my make-up brushes in half.
(He clearly was very strong and very enraged!)

My response was something like: You're pretty upset right now. What's bothering you? He was pretty verbal for a not-quite-two-year-old and you could almost hear his mind saying, "No shit, Sherlock!", but instead he said, "Take him out of here. Send him away." (Him being his new baby brother.)

I like to think that my response allowed him to feel his feelings and helped him learn ways to do so that WITHOUT breaking others' stuff or causing injury to yourself.

Unexpressed, unaddressed, unacknowledged rage wends its way into every aspect of our life and often comes out when we don't mean it to and with people who have little to do with this rage. Or if they do, it comes out as passive aggressive behavior because we don't acknowledge those darker feelings we feel.

Dive into the dark in order to receive and revive and live in the light…is how I'm beginning to see it now.

So, here's what we did on the retreat:

The women who wanted to, broke pencils with me.
The women who weren't ready or interested in doing so, took their pencil home as a reminder that they COULD—when/if they wanted to—break the pencil to express their rage.

It felt so liberating to do that.
It felt so freeing.

I felt so much lighter after I'd broken a few pencils.

Wanna break some pencils with me?

Many Blessings Always,

Paula

Just Sayin'

This morning, I sat on my glider…
to sit in stillness (aka meditate)
for 7 minutes because….

Because, well, 7 minutes
is what I can manage these days.

Oh! It's not just time.
It's the mind that flies from thing to thing.
It's my antsi-ness.
It's my judgement of myself.
It's what I can tolerate without sinking into lots of drama over "why can I no longer sit for longer than 7 minutes?"

Even though, intellectually I know that THIS IS THE PRACTICE—the jumping-bean mind and the catching of the jumping-bean mind—

I have SO much judgement of myself about this.

Some years back, I expressed this upset with my judgi-ness and a fellow yoga teacher
remarked, "You're a yoga teacher. You should know how to manage this monkey-mind."

Shame upon shame upon shame.

Isn't it enough that I'm a human being struggling with and/or confronted by my "monkey mind" as a bad, judge-able thing?

NO!

On top of that, we add, "You're a yoga teacher."

Implicit in this seems to be, "You're a yoga teacher and therefore better than this/You've mastered this or you should not be a yoga teacher."

That's how it came to me.

I shut down.

I cast no aspersions on this person, wondering about how honest and aware she was with herself and how much of her certainty was based on a profound desire for perfection in herself and others (Ask me how I know about THESE things!). No. I didn't question her assertion.

I withdrew to lick my wounds and hide in my shame.

Until…
My students continued to express their appreciation for my sharing my human-ness. And I heard them.

They told me that my vulnerability with them, that is my sharing my very real human experience of mind flailing, mind judging, falling over myself to get away from this monkey mind…made me a bridge for them, made it feel possible for them to access peace, calm, centeredness; made it ok that they couldn't do handstands in the middle of the floor and could still say that they practice yoga.

I have — over time and refining all the way — brought what was "out there"
and largely inaccessible to their real lives down to earth, to where we could all make sense as best we could, to where we were less afraid to try, and to where we could feel the benefits as they came to us, and not as someone else said they "should be."

Forty minutes of meditation?
How intimidating is this? How reachable is this?

But one minute? I can do that.
This is do-able and plants seeds for your sense of centeredness and calm.
And lo! and behold, one minute sometimes becomes 5.

"Do a little yoga, change a little. Do a lot of yoga, change a lot."

Au contraire, Maestro.

Our development is not linear as much as it is spirally.

And it all counts because YOU count. And "a little" becomes "a lot" in ways that are not necessarily quantifiable ways.

Can't manage a daily hour of yoga? ("can't manage" for ANY reason whatsoever — time, will, motivation, energy…) Do a pose here and there in your day.

Can't manage to devote your life to an ayurveda lifestyle? Choose ONE thing and do it

All that you do, do it with joy!

It all counts because YOU count.

Blessings,
Paula

Death's Smile

Thanks be to God, Alleluia.
Alleluia.
This is the song I woke to in my head.

Today,
I feel blank,
blanketed by a thick shroud
of heavy timelessness,
of life passing, flowing, pausing now and again
to genuflect
before the altar of the gods.

Which gods
is unclear.

The music within
swells.
The music within
abounds.
The music within
reassures
with its Presence,
and permanent impermanence,
with its silence
between the notes.

Life stands tall,

arms open,
in its certain uncertainty,
brilliant,
swathed in light and shadowy garments
of all hues,
textures,
weight.

Death smiles
its gentle,
knowing,
loving smile,
that we so often experience
as an evil smirk.

It's all there.
It's all here.

It's all within.

Grant me the peace
to receive it.

All.

Feeling and Trusting the Feelings...

I've been practicing and then teaching yoga for 25 years. One of the intentions of yoga is cultivating awareness… FEELING the body as it is right here, right now.

For someone like me who does a lot of thinking,
who spends a LOT of time in my head,
it's been an interesting journey.

Here's what I've come up with:

It's taken me most of these 25 years of practice to APPRECIATE how much I live in my head, how much I rely on my thinking cap
to create images for myself and my students
and how helpful this intellectual capacity has been….

except when it's gotten in the way of FEELING.

Which is a LOT of the time.

I have THOUGHT AND TALKED ABOUT feeling.
I have THOUGHT AND TALKED ABOUT how important it is that we LISTEN to our heart,
allow our intellect to SERVE our heart.
I have THOUGHT AND TALKED ABOUT AWARENESS of mind, body, spirt as one, inseparable.

It's been a lot of thinking.

What I've become aware of over the past couple of years is that my awareness has been more of an intellectual endeavor than an actual FEELING experience.

I'm sharing this with you, I'm being vulnerable with you because I KNOW that this is NOT an uncommon experience.

SO MANY OF US
think when we do well to feel.

SO MANY OF US
think RATHER than feel
because feeling opens up the gates of our personal history and it can be painful;

because feeling leads us into our heart and we've been taught from an early age not to trust our heart;

because feeling means receiving messages from our muscles and organs where we've stored the feelings for so many years (Bessel van der Kolk's book *The Body Keeps the Score* is one incredibly fascinating and affirming read!);

because feeling opens us to look at things we've been taught to or simply experienced feeling ashamed of;

because feeling scares us or annoys us or.

So often, my "feeling" was an intellectual exercise.

I believed that feeling was important, but I truly wasn't feeling so much as trying to feel and thinking I was feeling.

We can convince ourself of so much.

One of my favorite sayings is, "What people do and what people say they do are often very different things." Renowned anthropologist Margaret Mead was spot on, wasn't she?

We don't even know what we don't know.
We think we're doing X when we're really doing Y or maybe even Z.
We're not aware.
And we WANT to be aware (perhaps), but we don't know HOW to do things differently than we've been taught, or differently than we've been conditioned, or differently than we've habitually done them.

And, frankly, it's scary to step out of what we've been actually doing, especially when we THINK we've been doing something else.

It's been a journey…this recognition that I've been thinking more than I've actually been feeling.
It's been scary.
It's been filled with feelings that I've known intellectually. In my head, I had convinced myself that this was feeling.

It's not.
This doesn't make me (or you if this is true for you) wrong or bad or dishonest or…anything else.

It makes us human.

We do the best we know how.

And when we know differently, we practice doing differently.

So….Feeling the feelings…

Here are a couple of ways I have found to teach myself how to feel.

1. Sitting in stillness and continually drawing my attention back to what's happening, what I'm feeling in my physical body. 3-4-5 minutes is a great start. Anything more can become a fight. Become aware of the fight.

2. Choose a restorative pose (no stretching; no doing; just being!) and rest here for 10-20-30 minutes. Let yourself notice what happens with your body, with your thoughts. Notice without judging, without trying to change anything that's happening. The ONLY thing to change is when/if you become aware that something is physically uncomfortable. Change that! Go to: https://bit.ly/3zhXP1Z to see a video that I made of a restorative practice.

3. Pause here and there in your day to check in. WHAT are you feeling? WHERE? Notice, acknowledge and go on with your day…or notice what happens and what you change! Pausing has been shown to change our brain more than an action.

It's common and easy for us to turn away from the feelings. It's what society does. Feelings can feel dangerous.

I believe that it's only when we begin to feel our feelings that we're able to change our way of moving in the world.

Even the "ugliest" of feelings is not a truth. It's a feeling.

I hope you'll give yourself the gift of feeling YOUR feelings. And I'd feel honored if you'd share some of your experiences!

Blessings Always,

Paula

P.S. There's a LOT of feelings to uncover, explore, embrace, learn from, be curious about. May I offer that being curious about them helps us look without judging! May you be curious!

What's in YOUR Wallet?

Have I shared with you how there's a part of me that ABHORS technology—especially televisions, phones, and whenever my computer doesn't do something I thought I knew how to do?

Recently, I broke up with our television cable service (I know that just saying, "television cable service" dates me…because what other kind of cable service is there?)

I finally got so fed up with paying so much money per month when we really don't watch very much television and we only want it for occasional relaxing and March Madness basketball that I found the courage to do INTERNET ONLY and sign up with a streaming service.

OHMYGOD OHMYGOD OHMYGOD

I had said to my husband just three evenings prior, "There is nothing like the television and the phone to make me feel incredibly stupid."

And yet, here I was, gulping big gulps and walking into the Comcast store to say, "We're breaking up. Here's your stuff."

A lovely young woman, very empathic, talked me down from the ceiling and assured me that I'd be able to set up the streaming service and that there would be a discount for me for doing "internet only."

Well, the activation took 2 hours…and I had to remind myself, to just. keep. breathing.

I had to bat away all the nagging thoughts of, "SEE? You CAN'T do this. It's worth the extra couple of hundred dollars each month just so you don't have to feel so stupid."

I prevailed.

And THEN, I was able to select a streaming service AND GET IT GOING ON MY TV.

See? EveryDay Miracles really do happen!

I decided to use this entire experience and put it in my treasure trove (we could say file cabinet or rolodex, but then who would understand?) of things I've done that I help me develop my muscle of "I CAN. I HAVE. I WILL."

My ta-dahs.

My shining examples of "SEE? you CAN do hard things."

What's in YOUR wallet of hard things you've done to use as reference points when you're approaching yet another moment when you cringe at what it will take?

The "hard things" may not be hard for anyone but you.
No need to apologize or hide your head in shame because it appears easy for "them" and you're shaking in your boots as you even CONSIDER--

going to your first yoga class,

taking a water color art class when you've wanted to do so your entire life,
cooking for the first time what seems like a really complicated dish,
attending your first-ever retreat,
studying a second language,
starting your own business,
honoring your feelings when someone hurts them,
creating and holding boundaries for other people's behaviors in your presence,
crafting a letter of resignation,
traveling by yourself somewhere you've been before or NEVER been before,
asking a hard question of someone you love or someone you don't know…

What's hard for YOU? What would you LOVE to be able to do and you're so afraid that you can't make it happen/work/might screw up?

WE CAN DO HARD THINGS!

One teeny tiny itsy-bitsy step at a time.

I'm here to cheer you on!
I'm here to help you make ways and waves for yourself to honor yourself.

Please let me!

Many Blessings Always,
Paula

A Practice of Time

Do this with me.

"I have all the time in the world."

Say it out loud.
Say it out loud 3 times.
Say it out loud 3 times as you sit and wonder how you'll get it all done.

And then stop.

And in this pause,
Feel the freedom wash over and through you
As you know-all-over
The grace
Of being freed from the rush of time
Into the expanse of time.

"I have all the time in the world."

A Practice of Time
Part Two

Do this with me.

"I have reserved this space and time for me to breathe and be."

Say it out loud.
Say it out loud 3 times.
Say it out loud each and every time you experience the sensation that there is something else you "ought" to be doing instead of what you're doing right here right now that brings you pleasure, ease, comfort, joy.

Getting a manicure.
Getting a massage.
Walking by yourself for a mile or ten.
Swimming laps.
Reading a book.
Staring at the television.
Listening to music.
Playing golf.
Sitting in the warm sunshine.

"I have reserved this space and time for me to breathe and be."

Ahhhhhh…..

Brilliance

Soft
Silky
Velvety darkness

Starlight
Star Bright
First star I see tonight

May you soothe me with your
Grace-filled stillness
Comfort me with your soft silky caress
On my bare skin.

May you see me as I see you
Shining brightly and wide
Projecting your light onto shoulders and into the hearts
Of mice and men
Of doves and doers
Of sitters and walkers and runners and climbers
Of watchers and seers
Of listeners
Of singers and speakers..

Shower us all with your brilliance.
Out loud.
Whispering.
Screaming,

Crying.
Yelling.
Speaking.
Steady.
Wobbly.
Wavering in the moonlight.

Your brilliance is all around us
as your voice resonates within us
from you.
From deep within you.

Your authenticity inspires.
Your inspiration soothes.

Starlight
Star Bright.
Be the Star you are tonight.

Be the brilliance that you breathe.
Starlight
Star Bright.

Whose Voice Do You Hear?

For years, I've spoken to you loving words
So that you could hear my loving words
Until you replace them with your own.

For years,
I've spoken lovingly to you
So that you could hear and feel my
Loving tones
Until you replaced them
With your own loving, sweet tones

For years,
I've shared beauty with you,
Held up the mirror,
Encouraged you to look
From your loving heart through your loving eyes into your
    eyes and into your heart.

For years.

And all these words
All these loving tones
All this beauty and these loving eyes
Are now replacing me
With me.

I'm listening to what you have told me
Is my wisdom, my gifts,

My own beauty.

Thank you.
Bless you.
Love you.

We teach what we need to learn.

Yes! Oh! Yes!

Be kind to yourself.
See yourself with loving eyes

All these lessons
Knocking on my heart
As I shared them with you.
All these lessons now being welcomed in,
Beyond the foyer
And to the hearth,
The center of my deepest self
Where they have lain
Unearthed,
Stirred and shaken lightly
And now have caught fire.

Fan these flames.
I'm learning.

Sometimes, we hear our voice in the voices we use with others
    so that we can learn to hear our voices in and for our self.

Amen.

Club Baseball

When my sons played baseball and soccer,
Each sport had its season.
When that season ended,
We enjoyed other things and each other.

When I learned that
A coach had forbidden his players to go to a pool to swim and play during the hottest days of summer because they, then would be too tired for the evening, I knew that I'd been right to say, "Let's not."

Summer is for playing.

Period.

Not for performing.
Life is for playing, not for performing.

I don't want to rehearse life.

I want to live it.

When I'm Invited and I Cannot / Do Not Want To

I intend
to no longer use the phrase, "I have to."
when I'm asked to something that conflicts with plans
   already made.

I intend
to either say, "I get to."

OR

If "I get to" doesn't feel right to my heart,

I simply state what my plan is,
what I'm doing

OR

I simply say,
"I can't."

My heart is being liberated.
The simplicity of the plan
seems ingenious.

And a lifetime in coming.

Blocking Out the Other Voices

I have an image of a girl with her hands over her ears, closing her eyes because she wants to block out all the other voices, the other words, the other noises that seem to overtake and overrun her own thoughts, images, desires, words.

Martin Heidegger says that true listening is worship. May I add this: When you listen with your soul, you come into rhythm and unity with the music of the universe and you learn to experience yourself as one with that rhythm and unity. You learn to attune yourself to the silence and then to the whispers of your mind-body-spirit.

I'm inviting and urging you to listen deeply to your body's whispers, to your nudgings, so they don't become shouts

And if they become shouts?
Listen harder because the loudness means you haven't been paying attention.

And you are worthy of paying attention to.

Don't yet believe it?
This is ok.

Let the shouting begin.

Crying in the Shower Version 604A

I was tired.

I hadn't slept well.

I'd had a very full week...and still had more to do.

I'd been baking for a wedding shower all morning so I didn't walk,
didn't swim,
DID carve out time for a restorative practice, thank goodness.

And as I stood in the shower,
the tears began.

Over what, this time?
I wasn't sure.

I had been imagining all kinds of conversations with people all around my life,
especially siblings.

I felt anxious, lonely for my babies.
That is, lonely for the time when they were babies...
little guys who came in the middle of the night to snuggle because
they had a bad dream or woke up scared or...
needed my presence RIGHT next to them.

But today, I had just put contact lenses in my eyes and
this time, I said, "I'll wait to cry."
"I'll write about it and figure it out."

So minutes later, there I was, in full skirt, full makeup
(though I did leave off the mascara), standing in Dunkin' Donuts (Oops,
just Dunkin' now) when what song should come on?

Whitney Houston's rendition of Dolly Parton's "I will always love you."

Oh for goodness' sake.
These poor Dunkin' people kept stealing glances at me
as I let the tears stream out of my eyes and down my make-upped face.

Sigh.

It's a good thing that I have made peace with the fact that I cry easily.
Like at the drop of a note of...just about any song.

Even now, as I type these words, I hear Whitney's voice
and my eyes water, my throat closes.

Here they come again!
Truth.
Tears are always truth.

Many Blessings,

Paula

P.S. And then I discovered that I had two different (Unmatched) earrings in. That is worth a laugh or ten!

Was THIS why the the Dunkin' people were stealing glances at me?

Traveling Light

So this happened.

So I made this happen!

I chose to check my bag through to San Francisco instead of lugging it all over the airports and having to heave it up over my head when I got on the plane and then work hard to get it down without hitting someone on the head when I was getting off the plane.

I elected to NOT wear all my gear for the festival (because it takes up too much suitcase space and then I can't put it in the overhead compartment). In doing so, I chose a larger suitcase which would NEED to be checked.

I got anxious about having to figure out the kiosk to check the bag.

My husband dropped me at the airport and lo! And behold there were the guys who check your luggage curbside. Anxiety dismissed.

As I glided through security with only my beautiful leather backpack (my last birthday present to myself) and breezed through the terminal and easily found a seat without having to check the overhead compartment…I remembered…

THIS is my nod to slowing things down.
THIS is my way to meander and roam. I am unencumbered by this box being dragged behind and beside me. As I go in and out of shops, I'm unconcerned about knocking things off the shelf or rolling over someone's toes, of dislocating my shoulder.

I am free to move about the country, the world.

I am lighter.
I am slower.
I am thoroughly enjoying the light hearted-ness and the light weighted-ness of having only my backpack and waist belt.
I'm feeling joy in the slowing down and in the lightness, setting myself up for delight rather than hurry and heavy-ness.

I again trusted myself. Part of me wanted to "be practical." How is it practical to weigh one's self down with luggage?

Years ago, there was no carry-on culture. Years ago, the wait for the luggage was part of the journey.

I decided to listen—I wasn't in a hurry.
There was no need to rush through the airport, rush onto and off the plane, rush out of the airport.

In taking my time, I cared for myself, I set the pace for this trip, I again trusted, listened to, and honored my needs, my self.
I'm living the journey as it unfolds (Thank you Harold and your Purple Crayon.)
I'm helping this journey be a truer reflection of my truest self.

Even as the impatience of waiting waiting waiting for the luggage washed over me, I embraced it as part of the traveling, of my choice and decision to consciously SLOW. THINGS. DOWN.

Wow! Do I feel GREAT!

Join me in our quest to slow. life. down.

Blessings Always,
Paula

When the Pelvis Leads

After years of practicing with Judith Lasater, I began to better understand the links between the pelvis and the rest of our mind/body/spirit.

It is of critical importance to our health and well-being
that we appreciate the pelvis, specifically the pubic bone as the seat of our being;
the fulcrum of our life as we live it in the physical form and at the same time as we live through it in our spirituality.

The pelvis is the seat of our being.
We tilt it slightly forward to stand straight and tall.
Doing otherwise, gives us conflicting and confusing messages about who we are,
how we function, how we must proceed if we are to live on the outside what lies within us.

We tilt it slightly in and back when we are folding forward and when we are planking.

It's not meant to be the same movement all across the board. For everything we do, we would do well to listen to the body's wisdom instead of thinking we must direct this graceful, grace-filled holder of life.
Get out of the way.

Let the pelvis lead….

When the pelvis leads,
the legs follow and the feet follow the legs.
The knees, linking the two, feel safe.

When the pelvis leads,
the sacrum only moves as much as it was designed to move.

When the pelvis leads,
the spine follows, flows from and with its most natural rhythms.

When the pelvis leads,
we are ultimately able to find the path
that leads to our truest self,
to our heart of hearts.

Because when the pelvis leads
—and we follow—
we find and feel and live from a place of safety and centered-ness,
from strength.

When the pelvis leads,
We feel and feed our creativity in everything we do.

When the pelvis leads,
We stand tall in our true-ness,
empowered by the grace of our body, our mind, our spirit
as we consciously link them…
when the pelvis leads.

When the pelvis leads,

our heart opens wide with a spaciousness that clearly shows us
our sacred nature
of love and loving.

When the pelvis leads,
we speak our truth with gentleness and we are heard.

When the pelvis leads,
our mind serves our heart and our spirit.
We see clearly what is here and now
rather than what we wish for.

When the pelvis leads,
we are lifted up to the heavens
and we're able to live in the oneness that we are.

When the pelvis leads.

Many Blessings,

Paula

P.S. Want to experience how some movement feels with the pelvis leading? Go to https://bit.ly/3G1aREU

Finding My Voices

La la la la la la la.
Vocalizing.
Hearing voices that have changed over time.
Speaking Singing Shouting
Whispering the roles I've played in my life.

Mother. Daughter. Teacher. Wife. Writer. Singer.
 Cheerleader.
Barista. Swimmer. Runner. Coach. Walker. Piano player.
 Guitar player.
Reader. Observer. Participant. Hider. Shirker. Doer.
Mother of Babies, of Toddlers, of Teens, of Adults.
Listener. Speaker. Interrupter. Withdrawer.

These voices….
They're all mine.
Even the ones I don't especially care for,
even the ones that I feel ashamed of or embarrassed about.

They're all genuine.
(Even those that I pretend come from somewhere or
 someone else.)

They're all layered.
With age and experience
have nuances and subtleties as well as insights
that expand the range of these…voices.

The more deeply I've explored,
the more clearly I've seen.
The braver I've been in looking straight at it,
the better I've been able to disengage or refocus
to a different range or tone of voice.

I used to apologize for being everyone's cheerleader.
I used to deny my propensity to be positive and uplifting.
I fell into the trap
of negativity,
of sarcasm,
of the mode de jour—snarkiness.

Someone I love once called me a Pollyanna.
I shrunk.

If ogres have layers, so do voices.

And some are meant to be quiet.
Others are meant to be shared with great celebration.
All need to be acknowledged.
Perhaps healed or nurtured or edited or silenced,
redirected.

But they all need to be heard as existing
even when they serve better in silence.

Blessed Mother, Holy Spirit, Lord Jesus,
All the Angels and Saints, Holy Men, Women, and Children
open my ears and heart
to each and every of the voices that lie within me.

When a voice wishes to sing its joy,
let me get out of the way.

When a voice seeks to heal,
let me add soothing presence and perhaps actions to its
    softness.

When a voice from the past shouts for attention,
let me NOT turn away and deny or ignore it.
Instead, let me receive its pain
so that we may move forward and outward
and toward greater healing and joy.

When a voice of sadness begins lowing,
let me sit with its grief that it may heal
and wend its way into compassion.

When a voice of unsuppressed glee
begins turning cartwheels in my heart,
let me embrace her in her exuberance.

When a jaded, distraught voice happens to arise,
let me listen and learn.
And comfort if that seems to be what's needed.

Let me hear and listen to and embrace all the voices
in this chorus of my Being.

Let their harmonies, even the harsh harmonies,
be free to lilt across and into the wind,
joining their voices to those of the Universe.
where they came from to begin with.

Let us melt together into the One that we are.

Blessings.

Amen.

What Does A Woman Who Feels Worthy Do?

A woman who feels worthy…

…walks, heart lifted and open, eyes looking ahead, fully aware of her surroundings, taking it in. She walks with confidence, slow or fast, depending on her purpose and intention.
And she is ever aware of her purpose and intention.

She breathes evenly, aware of the impact of her breath on her body, her mood, how she speaks, how she projects herself to the world.

…seeks and cultivates and chooses beauty and grace in the world around her, in the forms that communicate beauty and grace to her.

Her voice is calm, full of her certainty, even in her uncertainty. It reflects her mindset that she can manage all that comes her way—good, bad, indifferent. It reflects her mindset that she is accepting of herself as she is, others as they are.

She raises her voice as necessary—in alarm, in passion, in excitement, in warning…

Her movements reflect her inner peace, her inner grace—whatever form they take, she's comfortable with them, unapologetic.

She stands in space, comfortable with taking up her space, even expanding outwards.

She looks into people's eyes when they speak and when she speaks AND when she listens. She knows that her presence makes a difference.

She discerns her hearts' desires and she does them, follows them, acts on them because, why not? They're hers and she's worthy of bringing them to life and light. She discerns and allows her priorities to make sense, to matter. She makes choices based on her priorities—whatever they are they reflect her at the moment and therefore, matter.

She acknowledges her feelings—whatever they are—without dismissing or apologizing.

She allows herself to be who she is. She allows others to be who they are and discerns with whom she wants to be.

She remembers the people who supported her, even inadvertently and she openly expresses her appreciation.

She expresses her rage by breaking pencils instead of heads, allowing herself to feel ALL the feelings, not just the pretty ones.

A woman who feels worthy…

…puts aside time, schedules time for herself to do what helps her relax and renew regularly, daily even.

She creates sacred space for herself, internally and externally

She sees her entire world (home and away) as reflecting her and takes steps to make it reflect what she wants to project into the world.

When she speaks, her words and demeanor reflect her centeredness, her beauty, her love.

She is steadfast, calm (even in expressing her passion), centered when she approaches challenging situations and people.

She behaves towards others with empathy, even in disagreement because she understands the internal dialogues and the emotions that lead people to their choices.

She is wholly herself, comfortable in her discomfort, able to laugh with herself and laugh with not AT others.

She doesn't need to say, "Fuck you" out of defense or proof…because she is so comfortable in herself that others' ideas simply bounce off her. Her warrior armor allows her to be as soft or hard as she is feeling. She chooses what she says based on the impact she wants to create.

She practices, exercises, displays herself as able and appropriate.

All of her self-awareness leads to self-ownership and continues to deepen her awareness.

She determines what's appropriate not from defiance or defense, but from her own centered self. She chooses how she wants to conduct herself in every situation because of or inspire of her feelings and knows why.

She dresses with care and intention to represent herself as she chooses.

Again, out of awareness and not defiance or if it IS defiance, she knows it and chooses it.

A woman who feels worthy...

...celebrates others' accomplishments, joys, new awarenesses, epiphanies, etc. with as much enthusiasm as she celebrates her own...

...celebrates her "ta-das" (from Jacqui)

...recognizes when she needs to lay low and does so without apology unless she recognizes that the other person needs (for whatever reason she deems important) to hear an apology

She reads people and situations with clarity and alacrity and insight..and chooses her responses to best fit her reading of the situation.

…says what needs to be said then stops, listens and watches, takes it all in.

…Acknowledges a mistake or mis-step or change of mind

…Sees or responds and apologizes unequivocally when she's hurt someone somehow any-how.

…Changes her mind without apology.

…Gives credit where credit is due for ideas, plans, itineraries, structures, words…

…Takes steps—little and big—toward what she believes or knows she wants.

…Operates under her own timing and without worrying about what others may think; acknowledges the worry, fear, and moves on to do what she can do when she can do it.

A woman who feels worthy…

…charts her own course, listens to others whose wisdom may enlighten her, but makes her own decisions so that they reflect exactly who she is and who she wants to be.

…accepts, embraces even that she will not have all the answers, that she can embrace the not-knowing, the feeling ill-at-ease as part of life

…asks for and receives support in whatever way she needs it in the given moment

…knows to care for her Inner Child, Inner Teen-ager, Inner Younger Version with the same grace and compassion as she cares for others

…attends to her nervous system so that she remains aware and cultivates resilience in her EveryDay life.

…practices daily/weekly/monthly/seasonally her rituals of action, of speech, of awareness.

…values Love above all else, no matter what maelstrom is going on around her. She speaks from love, looks from love, lives from love.

A woman who feels worthy…

…tells people with whatever manner she can muster when they have crossed a boundary she had set.

A woman who feels worthy…

…understands that others around her may occasionally look to her for guidance and support and doesn't hesitate to send someone home who doesn't know how to conduct him or herself in loving kindness of herself and the others…without rancor or apology or regret.

A woman who feels worthy...

>...holds her and others' boundaries to be sacred so she honors them with strength and compassion for all...

>...recognizes that many truths can be so at the same time and doesn't feel a need to embrace one at the expense of the other.

A woman who feels worthy…

>…is wholly herself…

Blessings Always,

Paula

Beauty Hunter

I wear a necklace to remind me.
I am a Seeker of Beauty, of Grace.
I am a Beauty Hunter.

In 2006, I took my sons to live in the south of France for 3 months.
We were blessed to rent a tiny (500 square foot) "Gîte" in a tiny town called Camaret sur Aigue.
We savored many walks along and in the dried-up bed of the River Aigue.
We played swords.
We played video games—the great uniter of boys across the planet.

And I saw beauty everywhere I went.

My sons were the first to point out how the light is different there than at home.
They were, of course, very right.
And I began looking for the light in every corner everywhere I went.

Days before we left to go home,
I took a walk around and into the town.
And I took photos.

My friend, the daughter of the people from whom we rented our "Gîte," paged through my scrap book of these photos and declared that she had never seen any of these things although her visits there were weeks-long and involved lots of walks.

"To see the beauty, you must expect the beauty to be there." Sometimes, the wisdom in my words surprises me.

But this rings true.
You must expect beauty.
You must be beauty.
You must recognize YOUR beauty.
You must be open to beauty…and grace.
All at the same time
because they play on and with each other
to create something even more beautiful than when they began.

Beauty.
It's here for us.
If we would but open our eyes and heart and being.

Join me.
Be a Beauty Hunter.
Seek the Beauty and Grace that lies within YOU
and you shall find the Beauty and Grace that lies all around you as well.

Turn away from the voices that tell you that Beauty is skin deep.
It is not.

Turn a deaf ear to the voices that proclaim that all the problems in the world deserve more attention than does Beauty or Grace.
They do not.

For, in Beauty,
in Grace,
we feel the presence of our truest nature,
we feel the presence of the Divine.
when we focus on this Divinity within ourself,
we are able to extend beyond ourself,
this appreciation for the Divinity that defines us…
when we allow it to define us…
when we choose to let Divinity, Beauty, Grace…
define us.

Look deep.
Look deeper.

See the light that shines.
In you.
From you.
All around you.
In them.
From them.
All around them.

Hunting Beauty
is one of the easiest things—and most delightful—
you can do for your self.

Echoes

Joining our voices in song or shouting,
whispering,
screaming, crying,
praying, cheering for…
creates a delightful cacophony,
a vibrant voice.

Join me in a rousing chorus of OM
and then stop.

In the silence,
you will hear the voices echo.

In the silence, you will feel
the beings behind the voices,
their love for you,
their love with you,
their love of you.

Close your eyes.
Or soften your gaze if closed eyes is too much for you right
 here right now.

You are safely held in the echoes of the songs of all of the
 loving
who came here before you,
of all of the loving who are with you today,

of all of the loving who are on their way,
some day.

Open your eyes
and bring forward and around,
the sense of one-ness with them,
all of them.

Feel the all-at-the-same-time-ness
of all of you,
of all of them.

Feel the tones,
the timbres,
the notes,
the half-steps,
the flats and sharps and dissonances and incredible
    harmonies
that dwell within all of the voices
and in which all of the voices dwell.

Be in harmony
with your voices.

They are all you.
They are all you being you.
Today.
Yesterday.
Tomorrow.

Your voice.
Your words.

Your voice in your words.
Your words in your voice.
Your voice beyond words.
Your words…beyond your voice.

Hear them in the echoes of your heart.

Listen.
Feel.
Let the tears stream down your cheeks.
Taste their salty sweetness.
Taste you.
Feel you.
Listen to you.
Be you.

Always.

Manifesto/Io Credo
(I believe. I know.)

For the last several years, thoughts have been bubbling in the back of my mind, urging me to put them on paper. Recently, the urge became an ache to create a document that shared what I believe, what's behind me, what's behind my business.

I didn't know what to call it. Manifesto seemed…hard. Credo grew on me because in Italian, "credo" is "I believe. I know."

Here's what my fingers placed gently on the page for me to share with you.

"It takes a lot of work to become, that is to feel and free all that you have always been, to breathe and to be. You are worth the work. You are worthy of being all of you. You are worthy." Paula Strupeck Gardner

I believe that everything in our life flows from this space in ourself of believing, feeling, *knowing* deeply that we are worthy. I believe that we **must feel safe and worthy** in order to feel truly at ease in our self, in order to pursue what we love and receive what we love, that this feeling of worthiness lives in our layers.

I believe we live in layers and that these layers are intertwined and intermingled; that as we learn and grow, we deepen, sometimes repeating similar lessons, but always to different levels and different layers of ourself.

"We are here to take care of each other; to do so, we must first take care of ourself." (Thich Nhat Han)

It is my raison d'être, my reason for being, to support you, cheer for you, celebrate you, encourage you, nudge you, love you as you find your way to you, as you navigate the steps and stumbles (which *are* among the steps) of your life.

I believe that the MindBodySpirit are, indeed, inseparable — what we do for (or to) one, we do for (or to) the others. Because of this inseparable-ness, we need to choose: words as well as foods and activities, how we speak to ourself as well as to others, how we care for our immediate environment (our home) as well as our world, how we rest because rest supports all of it.

I believe that the physical practices we actively engage in (yoga, walking-in-the-woods, tai chi, running, mudra, restorative yoga, healing sound, humming, chanting, etc), embody, support and are supported by the mind-work we do (active and seated meditations, word choice and thought reframing, writing our self, etc.). They feed each other.

I believe that when we see, accept, honor, and celebrate our body as sacred, when we celebrate what it has done and can do, we open our mind and heart to greater possibilities of being.

I believe that our layers shift and flow as we shift and flow; that there is no direct path, that each path is singularly ours and that everything along the way *is* a part of this path of ours.

I believe that when we become aware of our self, what and how and where in the body we feel what and all that we feel, we set the foundation for incredible joy.

I believe that when we trust ourself, our life expands, deepens, grows, shines in unexpected and delightful and glorious ways.

I believe that we can acquire the abilities to trust ourself, to care for ourself in as many ways as there are moments in a day, to live in beauty and joy; that our intention to become aware of our self, of who we were, who we are and who we want to be gives direction to our awareness and we are able, then, to deepen our trust in our self.

"Let the beauty we love be what we do." (Rumi)

I believe that our world—inside and outside—is filled with beauty, with wonder, with awe. And that we can expand our ability to see the beauty within us and around us with practices that work outside and inside. One supports the other and life becomes a beautiful upward spiral of beauty of all kinds.

"All holiness is about hearing the voice of your own soul." (John O'Donohue)

I believe that our voices speak our truths even in their silences, that we need not restrict ourself to having only one voice when we, in fact, may have many.

"Conformity is the last refuge of the unimaginative." (Oscar Wilde)

I believe that when we practice curiosity about the world and about ourself in the world, we have greater access to our truths and how we want to live them.

I believe that we can live "as though everything is a miracle." (Albert Einstein)

"How human of me." (Judith Lasater)

"Let no one ever come to you without leaving better and happier." (Sr. Teresa)

I believe that the MindBodySpirit holds infinite possibilities; that the shape of our life may be *interpreted* as behaving linearly—we are born; we live; we die—but that, in fact, we live in a circle of life and we are an integral part of this circle; that we do well to offer ourself and each other the grace and gift of compassion for ourselves as human beings "making our way home."

"If the only prayer you ever say is thank you, it would be enough." (Meister Eckhardt)

I believe in the power, the grace, the force of nature that gratitude is. I believe that the practice of gratitude enhances lives, sheds light on lives, saves lives.

I believe feeding our deep connections with Nature spreads the love; allows us to feel ever-deepening connections with our self and with others.

"Love is the bridge between you and everything." (Rumi)

"It all counts because YOU count." (Paula Strupeck Gardner)

I believe that everything we do matters deeply because we matter. Every little and every big thing we do counts.

I believe in celebrating.

"When you realize how perfect everything is, you will tilt your head back and laugh at the sky." (Unknown, often attributed to Buddha)

I believe in laughing at the sky.

I believe that we can live our life in love with life.

I believe giving credit where credit is due; by acknowledging where our inspiration had its roots, by celebrating each other's works and words, we open the sky. At the same time, when it doesn't matter who gets credit, we can accomplish so much more because our energy is directed to the doing.

I believe in the rule of Improvisational Theatre—"Yes…. AND…" instead of "Yes…but…" or "No…." or "but…."

I believe that all feelings from all sides are true at the same time.

I believe in you.

I believe that you're not likely to find anyone who sees you, hears you, loves you quite like I do.

Many Blessings,

Paula

Closing Notes

> "It took me quite a long time to develop a voice, and now that I have it, I am not going to be silent."
>
> *—Madeleine Albright*

May I offer you these thoughts from me and from others as you begin and continue your listening journey, as you pause to feel the resonance of *your* voices?

"When you begin dancing with the divine that is you,
You will find that your inner voice will get louder."
These are my words as repeated back to me by my Coach Jacqueline Gates.
I recorded them in a moment when I didn't quite believe or embrace.

You don't have to believe right now either;
I'm inviting you to believe that *I* believe.
I'm holding the space for your voice and your vision until you can step into them.

Practice when it's easy so that when you're in a tough moment, it's easy and/or feels natural to practice.

"The way we experience the world around us
is a direct reflection of the world within us." (G. Bernstein)

"The miracle comes quietly into the mind

when it stops for an instant and is still. " (A Course In Miracles)

You might ask yourself, in a moment of uncertainty,
"How would my *soul* tell the story? How would my *Inner Knowing* share these thoughts and feelings?"

You might be curious about:
Who am I? beyond my names, my roles, my doings?

We listen. We ponder. We discern. We resonate…or we do not and we honor whichever it is
because we listen to our Inner Knowing and we strengthen her voice each time we listen to her.

I look forward to welcoming you into my community,
into our chorus! Join us at www.YourVoicesYourTruths.com.

We need your voices.

Blessings Always,

Paula

Acknowledgements

I am so very grateful to my Teachers and Coaches over the years who drew and prodded and nudged my words from me before I knew they were there.

I am so very grateful to the Authors and Poets and all Writers I have read and loved over my lifetime. And while I never was blessed to meet them, I am especially grateful to Sister Macrina Wiedekehr, John O'Donohue, and Thich Nhat Han whose words not only lift my soul, but sing it as well.

I am grateful to Laura Jane Mellencamp Murphy who helped me find my voice as a yoga teacher, to Lori Gaspar who created what I needed, to the late and great Pat Layton whose knowledge of and experience with ayurveda and story-telling modeled both for my heart, to Judith Lasater whose voice and teachings challenge my status quo, to Julie Ann Turner who turned my ear and eye to my soul's longings, to Jacqueline Gates who continues to see through the veils and helps me be the Leading Lady of my own damn life, and grateful to Susan Quaid Brohan who instigated this journey when she held a metaphorical mirror before me and proclaimed, "YOU are a renaissance woman." And to my Dear Friend Mari, who paints me with such a loving brush that I can't resist the evidence.

I'm grateful for my husband who, though the whispers, screams, and crying out loud may make him want to race for cover, stands at my side no matter what, for my sons who are forever my heart living outside my body and for my daughter-in-law whose steadfast presence in my son's life tells me that all is right with the world.

Where would I be without the Angels?
Where would I be without the memories of my Dad?

I'm grateful to the world's best formatter in Debbie Lum (Contact her at debbie@debbiestevenlum.com). And to the world's best cover designer in Danijela Mijailovic (Reach her at lila.mijailovic@gmail.com). And hoping they're around for all the rest of my books!

Where would I be without YOU dear reader, dear whisperer, dear screamer?
Where would I be without YOUR VOICES?

I thank you all for being here and for sharing your voices, your truths.

P.S. To reach Julie Ann Turner, go to www.RenaissanceGenius.com

To reach Jacqueline Gates, go to https://www.jacqueline-gates.com/

About the Author

Wife, Mom, Teacher, Author, Coach, Retreat Guide…

One of Paula's favorite voices has been the one who said this:

"I may have an impressive resume that includes advanced degrees and certificates. And even though, I am the first-ever US woman to have completed the Mt. Everest Marathon (1989), and even though I've done things, lived things, created, written and published things, led retreats and coached people everywhere, taught for 40+ years, etc. etc.,

I want you to know **this** about me:

I care about you. Deeply. I cheer for you. Loudly and with unmatched enthusiasm. I am the staunchest supporter you'll ever have, the most loving mirror you'll ever look into, the most transparent, unflinchingly authentic voice you'll ever hear…

As I hold space for you to do the same for you…"

Join me in all the ways you can.

Blessings,
Paula

You're Invited...!

I'd love to hear from you!

I love to know how my words resonate with you.

Would you please take a moment to write your honest review of this book?

Go to Amazon and Barnes and Noble to leave your review.

I appreciate your taking the time.

And then, come join my community by entering your name and email address at www.YourVoicesYourTruths.com

Blessings Always,

Paula

P.S. You can find my other books on Amazon and Barnes and Noble, too!

Wrapping My Fears in Wonder: EveryDay Prayers to Help You Find, Feel, and Be Calm, Resilient, and Healthy of Mind, Body, and Spirit

MS Chair Yoga At Home: Your Step-By-Step Guide 25 Poses to Alleviate Tension, Tightness, & Anxiety So You Can Thrive!

www.ingramcontent.com/pod-product-compliance
Lightning Source LLC
Chambersburg PA
CBHW071859070526
44583CB00016B/1754